Halloween Jack-o'-Lanterns

BY KATHRYN STEVENS

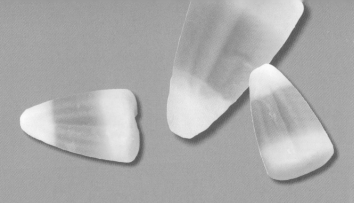

The Child's World®

Published by The Child's World®
1980 Lookout Drive • Mankato, MN 56003-1705
800-599-READ • www.childsworld.com

ACKNOWLEDGMENTS

The Child's World®: Mary Berendes, Publishing Director
The Design Lab: Design
Olivia Gregory: Editing
Pamela J. Mitsakos: Photo Research

Design elements ©: Natalya Aksenova/Dreamstime.com:
candle; Vlue/Shutterstock.com: candy corn; Zamlunki Tree/
Shutterstock.com: leaves
Photographs ©: Bartkowski/Dreamstime.com: 15; Chepko
Danil Vitalevich/Shutterstock.com: 7; Ilike/Shutterstock.com:
13; IndigoLT/Shutterstock.com: 11; mikeledray/Shutterstock.
com: 19; monkeybusinessimages/iStock.com: 9; sonyae/iS-
tock.com: 21; Stuart Monk/Shutterstock.com: 17; tshortell/
iStock.com: 4-5; Yellowj/Shutterstock.com: cover, 1

ISBN 9781631437458
LCCN 2014945408

Printed in the United States of America
Mankato, MN
November, 2014
PA02244

Table of Contents

It's a Jack-o'-Lantern!

You are walking along on a windy night. You see two eyes and a mouth glowing in the darkness. You look closer at the glowing face. It has a gap-toothed grin. Yellow light shines through its huge eyes. What is this strange sight? It's a jack-o'-lantern!

You have probably seen jack-o'-lanterns when you were trick-or-treating. You might have even carved one yourself.

What Is the Origin of Jack-o'-Lanterns?

The **origin** of jack-o'-lanterns comes from an Irish folktale. The story is about a **stingy** man named Jack. Jack made a deal with the Devil. Heaven would not take Jack when he died. Neither would the Devil! Jack's ghost wandered the earth with a lantern. Jack became known as "Jack of the lantern."

There are many different types of jack-o'-lanterns. Some have spooky faces and sharp teeth. Others just look silly.

How Did Halloween Get Started?

Halloween comes from very old **traditions**. Different **cultures** had festivals to honor their dead. Many people believed that the spirits of the dead came back during the festivals.

These festivals turned into Halloween. Halloween is now a fun autumn **holiday**. We decorate our homes and have parties to celebrate.

Halloween parties can be a lot of fun. They are filled with costumes, games, and candy.

Why Do We Have Jack-o'-Lanterns on Halloween?

People used to be afraid of spirits on Halloween. They tried to frighten the spirits away by dressing in costumes. They also set out lanterns with carved faces. They made the lanterns by carving out turnips and placing candles inside. These carved **turnips** were the first Halloween jack-o'-lanterns.

We still dress in Halloween costumes today. We do not do it to scare away spirits, though. We do it to get candy!

Why Are Jack-o'-Lanterns Made from Pumpkins?

Irish settlers brought the story of Jack and his lantern when they came to North America. They also brought their Halloween traditions. But North America had few turnips for making carved lanterns. The new settlers used pumpkins instead. They discovered that pumpkins were not as solid as turnips. Their insides were easier to scoop out for holding candles.

Pumpkins are filled with seeds. You can start carving once you take the seeds out.

13

What Are Pumpkins?

Pumpkins are a kind of squash. There are many different kinds of squashes. Zucchini and acorn squash are just two examples.

Pumpkins are actually the fruits of pumpkin plants. The seeds for making dozens of new plants are inside each pumpkin.

Squashes come in many sizes, shapes, and colors. Many of them are good to eat.

How Else Can Pumpkins Be Used?

Pumpkins are also very good to eat! Large pumpkins are often tough and dry. But smaller ones are tasty and tender. They are good for making pumpkin pie.

Some people save pumpkin seeds when they carve jack-o'-lanterns. These seeds make a tasty snack when they are roasted.

Pumpkin pie is a traditional fall dessert. Many people like to eat it on Halloween and Thanksgiving.

What Do Pumpkin Plants Look Like?

Pumpkin plants have great big leaves. They also have winding stems called **vines**. Pumpkin vines can grow longer than 10 feet (3 m). They can take over a small garden! Some gardeners make their plants grow up fences instead of spreading all over the ground. Others just let their plants run wild!

It can be fun to grow pumpkins in a backyard garden. Then you can carve them into jack-o'-lanterns!

How Big Can Pumpkins Grow?

The biggest pumpkin ever grown weighed 1,140 pounds (517 kg)! It takes lots of work to grow a pumpkin that big. You need to use lots of **fertilizer**.

Take a close look at the jack-o'-lanterns you see when you are trick-or-treating. They are all saying one thing: "Have a Happy Halloween!"

Some pumpkins are gigantic. Just think of the jack-o'-lantern you could carve from a pumpkin this big!

GLOSSARY

cultures (KUHL-churz) Cultures are the histories, beliefs, and practices of different groups of people.

fertilizer (FUR-tuh-lye-zur) Fertilizer is the food a plant uses to grow. Giant pumpkin plants need a lot of fertilizer.

holiday (HOL-uh-day) A holiday is a special day that people celebrate every year. Halloween is a holiday.

origin (OR-uh-jin) The beginning of something is called its origin. The origin of the Halloween jack-o'-lantern lies in an old Irish folktale about a man named Jack.

stingy (STIN-jee) Stingy people hate to spend their money or give it away. Jack-o'-lanterns are named after a folktale character who was stingy and mean.

traditions (truh-DISH-uhnz) Traditions are ways of doing things as people have done them for a long time. Our Halloween celebrations include many old traditions.

turnips (TUR-nuhps) Turnips are vegetables with round, whitish roots that you can eat. Long ago, Irish people made lanterns by carving out turnips and putting lights inside them.

vines (VYNZ) Vines are long, weak-stemmed plants that climb up things or creep along the ground. Pumpkins grow on large vines.

BOOKS AND WEB SITES

BOOKS

Blue Lantern Studio. *The Truth about Jack-O-Lanterns*. Seattle, WA: Laughing Elephant, 2006.

Heiligman, Deborah. *Celebrate Halloween with Pumpkins, Costumes, and Candy*. Washington, D.C.: National Geographic Children's Books, 2007.

Robbins, Ken. *Pumpkins*. Milford, CT: Roaring Brook Press, 2006.

WEB SITES

Visit our Web site for lots of links about Halloween jack-o'-lanterns:

childsworld.com/links

Note to Parents, Teachers, and Librarians: We routinely verify our Web links to make sure they are safe, active sites—so encourage your readers to check them out!

INDEX

ABOUT THE AUTHOR

Kathryn Stevens has authored and edited many books for young readers, including books on animals, countries, holidays, and instruments. A resident of La Crosse, Wisconsin, Kathryn is a lifelong pet lover and currently cares for a big, huggable pet-therapy dog named Fudge.